P9-DID-395

Impressions of
PRINCE EDWARD COUNTY

The Island County
of Ontario

Photographs by
Sue Cory

CORY CARDS AND PHOTOGRAPHS
PICTON, ONTARIO 1990

Design: Sue Cory
Photography: Sue Cory
Production: Joe Cembal, Jr.
          Prince Edward Printing
Publisher: Cory Cards and Photographs
          R.R. 4
          Picton, Ontario
          K0K 2T0
ISBN 0-9694600-0-7
Copyright 1990 Sue Cory
          All rights reserved. No part
          of this publication may be
          reproduced by any means
          without prior written consent.
Cover Photo: Glenora Ferry with Sumac from Lake-on-the-Mountain
Printed in Canada

To Norm
for his unfailing
support and encouragement

This collection of photographs
is a tribute to the beauty, variety,
mystery and magic of Prince Edward County.

Sue Cory, 1990

2. Schoolhouse at Bowerman's Corners

1. Spring Flooding on Gomorrah Rd.

3. Waterfall—Cape Vesey

4a. Maple Syrup Time—East Lake

4b. Rural Mailboxes—Hallowell

5a. Schoolhouse—Long Point

5b. Cedar Log Building—Long Point

6. Red Bush on a Gravel Beach at Gull Bar

7. Early Spring in the Marsh—Gull Pond

8. Barn with Double Silo—Albury

9. Silo on Burr Rd.

10. Cemetery and Church near Niles Corners

11. Back Gate to Rose Cemetery

12. Early Morning on Smith Bay from Stevens Lookout

13. Birch Tree by Smith Bay

14. Cedar Corral on Bradley Crossroad

15. Horse Barn on Hiway 33 and Hubb's Creek Rd.

16. Glenora Fisheries

17a. Glenora Stone Mills

17b. Glenora Reflections

18. Red Barn at Glenora

19. Orchard at Waupoos

20. Pear Tree—Waupoos

21. The Old Cannery at Waupoos

22. Log Cabin at the Ameliasburg Museum

23. Red House with Spirea—Ameliasburg

24. The Pond at Harry Smith Conservation Area

25. Flowers by the Stream at Demorestville

26a. Lilacs and White Barn—Bongard

26b. The House in the Lilacs—Cressy Bayside

27a. Lilacs by a Forgotten Hideaway on County 14

27b. Lilacs by an Abandoned House—Sophiasburgh

28a. Flowers on the Cliffs at Pt. Petre

28b. Rocks and Flowers at Pt. Petre

29. Black Rock—Pt. Petre

30a. Log Cabin Point at East Lake and the Outlet River

30b. Cabins on the Outlet River

31. A Quiet Day at West Point

32. Lake Ontario at Peace

33a. Tree on the Sandbanks Beach

33b. The Outlet Beach

34. The Dam at Consecon

35. Consecon Feed Mill

36. Baldwin Milling, Ltd near Consecon

37. The Old Train Station near Consecon

38. Relics of the Past on a Sheep Farm at Fish Lake

39. Antique Tractor in a Field near Black Creek

40. Rusted Pump by an Abandoned House—N. Marysburgh

41. The Wycott House near Black Creek

42a. Farm House on Hiway 33 West of Bloomfield

42b. Dairy Farm on Hiway 33 West of Bloomfield

43. Farm on the Outskirts of Picton

44. The Cement Plant by Picton Bay

45. Sunset on Picton Bay

46. A Field near Hillier

47. Hayfield on Hiway 62

48. The Bridge over the Telegraph Narrows

49. The Shore at Rossmore and Bridge to Belleville

50. Flowers by Hayward Long Reach

51. Split Rock on a Hillside by Long Reach

52. Willow Tree at Massasagua Point

53. The Birch Tree at Little Bluff

54a. Picton's Crystal Palace

54b. The Church at South Bay

55. Bethesda Community Hall

56. Waterfall near Scott's Mill

57. Fieldstone Grave Marker at Chadsey Cemetery

58. Sunset on Weller's Bay

59. Boats in Black Creek

60. Wellington Harbour

61. Cattails by Prinyer's Cove

62a. Cornfield on the Ridge Road

62b. Grimmon's Woods

63a. Boat Dock—Cherry Valley

63b. Boat by the Bay of Quinte at Carrying Place

64. Windy Day at Pt. Petre

65. Lighthouse—Pt. Petre

66. Milford Mill Pond

67. Picton Harbour

68. Autumn at Black Creek

69. Trees on a Small Island near Glenora

70. Small Shed Peeking Through Sumac—N. Marysburgh

71. Autumn Splendor—N. Marysburgh

72. Pumpkin Patch by Athol Bay

73. Shed—Cherry Valley

74a. Soybean Field on Hiway 62 near Bloomfield

74b. Farm on Gore Rd.

75a. Corn Crib—Ameliasburgh

75b. Gingerbread Barn—Ameliasburgh

76. The White House on the Hill

77. Old Tractor Hiding in a Shed

78a. Dunes by West Lake

78b. Beach by West Lake

79a. Dunes and Sky—Sandbanks Prov. Park

79b. Dead Cedars in the Sandbanks

80a. A Door to the Past

80b. Blue Windows

81. The Checkerboard House

82. Patterns in the Sand Dunes at North Beach

83a. Trees on North Beach

83b. Wave Breaking on North Beach

84. Lake Ontario in December

85. Lighthouse—Prince Edward Point

86. Woods in Winter—Pt. Petre

87. Glazed Dunes at the Outlet Beach

88. The Channel at Wellington

89. Winter Sun—Huyck's Point

90. Barn in a Snowstorm—N. Marysburgh

91. Lone Tree in a Field of Blowing Snow—N. Marysburgh

92. Iced Cliffs—Pt. Petre

93. Iced Trees by Prince Edward Bay—Long Point

94. Snow on the Dunes—Sandbanks Prov. Park.

95. Lighthouse—Salmon Point

96. Winter Sun—Pt. Petre

Glenora—Winter

ISBN 0-9694600-0-1